The Soul of Peaceful Living
Reflections for Transformation

~ Gena Livings ~

The Soul of Peaceful Living: Reflections for Transformation

Copyright © 2017 Gena Livings

All rights reserved. No portion of this book may be reproduced mechanically, electronically, or by any other means, including photocopying, without written permission of the author. It is illegal to copy this book, post it to a website, or distribute it by any other means without permission from the author.

"The Soul of Peaceful Living", "Reflections for Transformation" are TradeMarks of Gena Livings.

ISBN: 978-0-9826193-2-2

Gena Livings
Gena@GenaLivings.com
GenaLivings.com

Cover art by lumix2004 courtesy of Pixabay
Author photo by Marie Clark

Acknowledgments

I give thanks unceasingly to our Heavenly Creator; the source of all life and love.

I would like to express my deepest gratitude for my mom and dad. Although they have transitioned from this physical world, they continue to guide my way and support my passage. I give never-ending thanks to my husband, Bob, for loving, supporting and believing in me always. I am also extremely grateful for my friends and family who have all deeply blessed my life with their special wisdom, beauty and grace.

God continues to bless me with angels and teachers who inspire me to live my best life and think my best thoughts in the Spirit of love and light. I would also like to take the time and acknowledge them here because without their influence, this book would not be possible.

My personal mentor and spiritual life coach – Bob. Teachers and authors: Joyce Meyer, Dan Millman, Marianne Williamson, Wayne Dyer, Jack Canfield, Florence Scovel Shinn, Brene Brown, Gary Zukav, Robin Sharma, Sierra Bender, Dina Dove, Mark Nepo, Abraham Hicks, Janet Nestor, Rick Warren,

Louise L. Hay, Neil Donald Walsch, and the work of Katie Byron.

My deepest appreciation for my editor, Sandy Scherschligt, for her continued support, perspective and helpful guidance. Sandy has graciously supported me through each and every book project that I've brought into existence. She has been one of my greatest blessings. Thank you, Sandy for everything!

I would also like to acknowledge the following people for their loving assistance in the creation and distribution of this book: Dina Dove for providing the introduction to this book and being an inspiration to myself and many others. The amazing Laurie Tossy for her creative insights, book design, publishing support and guidance. De Harris for her ongoing technical, strategic, administrative support and guidance. Bonnie Gortler for always being my greatest supporter and biggest fan.

I am blessed and I am grateful beyond measure.

Gena Livings

Foreword

For years I wished I had the 'Cliff Notes' version of the most empowering Biblical quotes that pointed the way to a life of joy and fulfillment.

Having made several attempts to read the Bible from cover to cover, I always get lost in the challenging language, the names I could not pronounce, and the overwhelming size of the undertaking. Even so, I have always been confident that the highest truths were "in there somewhere".

Here they are. We finally have them at our fingertips.

The Soul of Peaceful Living: Reflections for Transformation

Great books for me are those that have a big impact with a small time commitment. This one does just that with the ability to spend 10-15 minutes a day basking in one reflection at a time. When we add the most powerful truths of life to our daily regimen, positive change happens.

The simple truth is that God desires to give us the kingdom, if we will but ask it of Him.

So many times, instead of asking for that which will bring us the greatest joy, we assume that the new car, the position on an influential board, or acceptance into the right university is what dreams are made of. And we can end up trading Heaven for things of earth.

Do not buy into the myth that if you put God first that your life here on earth will lack luster. That is completely opposite of the divine reality. When you are in alignment with your soul's highest calling, you will effortlessly bring more beauty and joy to the world.

Jesus's attention was always focused on God, and that is the example we should imitate. When we do that, the Kingdom is ours. Joy, peace, fulfillment and Heaven can be experienced right here, right now.

One has only to look at the smile of a child, a beautiful sunset, a blossoming flower – who could deny the potential to experience it all as Heaven. But in order to attain it, you need to take time to nurture your soul and discover peaceful living within. God needs us to step up, to shine our light brightly.

Looking back on the most profound truths of life, one thing quickly comes to mind. They are simple and straightforward. It is we who make life complex by one major misconception. <u>Over thinking</u>.

We cannot imagine that the key to happiness and a life that works doesn't require all kinds of machinations and efforts.

You know the old saying, "You get what you pray for".

Well, my prayer has been answered and yours too. Thank you, Gena Livings for your inspiring new life changing guide: *The Soul of Peaceful Living.*

Dina Dove

Author

Baglady's Guide to Elegant Living: Learn to Love the Life You Have

From the Author

*When our mind is healthy,
so is our Soul.
~ Gena Livings*

The Soul of Peaceful Living: Reflections for Transformation is a heartfelt collection of practical and positive insights that can transform your life from the inside out.

The goal of **Peaceful Living** is something that we all strive for in our **soul** but so many of us struggle with this because of the negative thought patterns that habitually run through our mind.

As a spiritual practitioner of peaceful living, I have made it my single-minded purpose to focus on thoughts that bring forth a peaceful life in the spirit of love, light, and truth.

The Soul of Peaceful Living is a form of creative expression and is intended to foster a positive mindset and bring forth feelings of peace, joy, and love.

I specifically chose the format in this book to share my personal reflections with you. Each of these reflections includes a pivotal biblical passage. I sourced scriptures from various English translations of the Bible. These passages were the ones that worked deep within my spirit, and guided me to discover the soul of peaceful living by asking myself the question:

"How can these passages help me change my thoughts to experience inner peace?"

I pass these along to you as an opportunity to reflect upon them. I believe these inspirations will touch your soul as well. The idea is not to merely read these words but to spend quiet time with each reflection and allow them to penetrate your daily life.

Healthy Blessings,

Gena Livings
Spiritual Practitioner of Peaceful Living

Introduction to Mindful Reflection

I have discovered that we often live enslaved by our minds, thoughts, belief systems, mental patterns and emotions. We have a tendency to resist changing for the better out of our own egocentric control to be in charge. When we are willing to let go of our need to control everything, we allow the spirit of God/Love to transform us for the better. When we do this, we also let go of looking to the world as our source of well-being and happiness.

The good news is that with some self-awareness and effort, we can begin to free ourselves from the negativity of our mind and enter into the mind of God (Love).

Our thoughts affect us in so many ways and they help us create the reality in which we experience daily life. Whether that experience is good or bad, all of it is determined by our thoughts, how we interpret those thoughts and perceive the world around us.

Everything we do and produce in this world stems from our thoughts. Our thoughts turn into feelings, which turn into actions and our actions are what ultimately produce our outcomes.

When our thoughts are aligned with our Creator, we experience a world that feels peaceful, loving and kind. When our thoughts are burdened with negativity, we experience a world that feels fearful, anxious and full of worry and stress.

I believe negative thinking is a learned behavior that was acquired over time through many generations and outside influences that were not in alignment with the Spirit of Love (God). The good news is that any thoughts that are learned can also be unlearned when we develop a God (Love) Centered Mindset. This is often referred to as The Christ Mind or Christ Consciousness.

When we focus our attention on positive (God Thoughts) instead of negative fear based thoughts, our mental, physical and emotional health improves immensely. This is because positive thoughts create healing and produce the feeling of joy in our lives. Plus, positive thoughts reduce stress and anxiety in our lives.

When our thoughts are infused with God Thoughts, we will experience perfect peace instead of anxiety, fear and worry.

In order for us to live a happy, healthy and

fully productive life, we must be willing to transform our fear based thoughts into positive thoughts centered in love and emotional well-being.

May the reflections and biblical passages in this book strengthen, heal and nurture your soul in the spirit of love, light and inner peace.

Do not conform to the pattern of this world, but be transformed by the renewing of your mind. ~ Romans 12:2

Reflections

We all have the power within to crush Goliath (our giant fears) when we arm ourselves with a positive mindset.

So David triumphed over the Philistine with a sling and a stone; without a sword in his hand he struck down the Philistine and killed him. ~ 1 Samuel 17:50

To enter the realm of perfect ideas (God's Kingdom), where miracles happen, we must see the world through the eyes of children.

This is because little children are open channels to receiving all that is good. They have a "Miracle Consciousness" and are filled with expectation in a world where all things are possible with God (Love). They don't allow fearful thinking and doubt to cloud their sense of wonder. They expect only the good.

When Jesus saw this, he was indignant. He said to them, "Let the little children come to me, and do not hinder them, for the kingdom of God belongs to such as these."
~ Mark 10:14

When we place our faith in Love (God), we place our faith in only one power. So, place your faith in Love and thoughts of fear disappear.

I sought the LORD, and he heard me, and delivered me from all my fears.
~ Psalm 34:4

Let your every thought and your every word be an expression of the Eternal Light within you.

Death and life are in the power of the tongue.
~ Proverbs 18:21

When you begin to recognize all of your negative thoughts – your vision (perception) becomes clear and all false impressions are dissolved and absorbed into the light of healthy perception.

The eye is the lamp of the body. If your eyes are healthy, your whole body will be full of light. ~ Matthew 6:22

What we truly feel from the depths of our heart will eventually transpire in our daily life. When we focus our attention (our thoughts) on the good by finding a positive meaning in all things, all good things come to pass in the heart of our daily affairs.

Keep thy heart with all diligence, for out of it are the issues of life. ~ Proverbs 4:23

The perfect you IS the Love that is found within you. Love isn't material, it's energy. It's not seen with your eyes or heard with your ears, it's intuitive and felt within your heart.

The Kingdom of God is within you.
~ Luke 17:21

Negative thinking creates a separation from God (Love) and our Source of well-being (heaven from within). When we are saved through the energy of Love, our minds and thoughts are restored from all negative perception. Peace and well-being become our Paradise and our new Perception.

Jesus answered him, "Truly I tell you, today you will be with me in paradise."
~ Luke 23:43

When you choose to align your Will (Love) with Gods Will (Love), you create an eternal Love Connection.

For it is God who is at work in you, both to will and to work for His good pleasure.
~ Philippians 2:13

When we ask God (Love) to transform our lives, we are saved from our negative and fearful thinking to a more peaceful, positive and loving perspective. We now perceive love and well-being as our only function.

And Peter said to them, "Repent and be baptized every one of you in the name of Jesus Christ for the forgiveness of your sins, and you will receive the gift of the Holy Spirit." ~ Acts 2:38

With the multitude of challenges (love lessons) we face in this lifetime, the Infinite Intelligence (God) provides a channel (a way) for us to acquire the skills we need to fulfill our life purpose. These love lessons build upon each other to strengthen our character (heart) and our ability to serve a Higher Purpose with great joy and inner peace!

Dear brothers and sisters, when troubles come your way, consider it an opportunity for great joy. For you know that when your faith is tested, your endurance has a chance to grow. So let it grow, for when your endurance is fully developed, you will be perfect and complete, needing nothing.
~ James 1:2-4

It's time to Wake Up from your dead-end thinking (your self-doubt, your insecurities, your fears, your worries and all your limiting beliefs).

The Love within you gives RISE to a New Light (understanding) and a new perspective (Life). See to your radiance, your beauty, your full potential and your unbounded splendor. Ascend to your Highest Good!

Awake, O sleeper, rise up from the dead, and Christ will give you light.
~ Ephesians 5:14

When we say a prayer over our food, we are naturally in a positive state of mind and centered in a loving heart. The feeling of gratitude and appreciation brings the energy of God (Love) into our food and therefore into our body.

So, whether you eat or drink, or whatever you do, do all to the glory of God.
~ 1 Corinthians 10:31

Prayer before a meal is a time of letting go of the day and being in the present moment with complete awareness and gratitude for the gift of food. Use this time to be present and conscious of not only the food you are about to eat but the blessing of sharing a meal with those you love.

When we ask a blessing over our food, we honor God by acknowledging His provision.
~ Psalm 50:23

When you eat the whole natural foods that God (Love) intended, your immune system will be strong and your hormones will be in balance. This intended way of eating allows your body to fight off toxins from the environment and food contaminants you consume.

God (The Infinite Intelligence) does not want to see our bodies suffer by becoming sick and diseased from all our unhealthy food choices.

Beloved, I pray that you may prosper in all things and be in health, just as your soul prospers. ~ 3 John 1:2

Your body was made to be active! It was not designed to stay still. It needs to MOVE around. Exercise is incredible for helping overcome depression and self-confidence issues. As you move your body, you get healthier and stronger. Then your mind starts seeing everything, including yourself in a more positive light.

Since we are living by the Spirit, let us follow the Spirit's leading in every part of our lives.
~ Galatians 5:25

I Believe WE can stop focusing on our individual needs and open our "One Heart" to the greater good, to choose what will benefit ALL.

I believe WE can realize that in this intertwined world, if the least among us benefit, we all benefit. If they suffer, we all suffer.

I believe WE can let go of our need to blame, to judge, to scapegoat – all the thoughtless and hasty ways we separate ourselves from each other.

I believe we can SHIFT away from competition, self-centeredness, self-interest and self-protection. And do this in all areas of our life – at work, at home and in our public affairs.

I believe WE can give up FEAR and exchange it for Generosity, Unity and Love.

Be completely humble and gentle; be patient, bearing with one another in love. Make every effort to keep the unity of the Spirit through the bond of peace. There is one body and one Spirit, just as you were called to one hope when you were called; one Lord, one faith, one baptism; one God and Father of all, who is over all and through all and in all.
~ Ephesians 4:3-7

The ability to love oneself is the core and foundation of our ability to love others and to love God. When you practice self-love, you send a message to the Universe that you are worthy. In fact you are a divine being! Not to love yourself is to deny your own spirit.

You must love the Lord your God with all your heart, all your soul, all your strength, and all your mind. And, Love your neighbor as yourself. ~ Luke 10:27

Forgiveness is a daily practice that becomes easier in time. You will slowly build the habit of letting go of anger and focusing your attention on a more peaceful and loving perspective.

Hatred stirs up strife, but love covers all offenses. ~ Proverbs 10:12

Be friendly to everyone around you. Kindness is UNCOMPLICATED. You can PRACTICE it anywhere, anytime.

Be kind to one another, tenderhearted, forgiving one another, as God in Christ forgave you. ~ Ephesians 4:32

Choosing to be grateful for all our outcomes is a "choice" and a "habit" that we consciously form over time with practice. When we consciously practice being grateful for the people, situations and events in our life, we eventually begin to "attract" better outcomes.

The practice of being thankful will be strengthened (like strengthening a muscle) as you make the choice each day to incorporate gratitude as a way of "being." This is the first step towards healthy emotional and mental well-being.

And let the peace of God rule in your hearts, to which also you were called in one body; and be thankful. ~ Colossians 3:15

Be still. You must choose to slow down, quiet your mind and be at peace before you will hear the Spirit of God (Love) within you.

The wind blows where it wishes, and you hear its sound, but you do not know where it comes from or where it goes. So it is with everyone who is born of the Spirit.
~ John 3:8

No matter what happens in your life today, TRUST that all is GOOD and unfolding in your BEST interests. You are exactly where you are meant to be on your path in this very MOMENT. Are you ready to let go and let Love?

Trust in the Lord with all your heart, and do not lean on your own understanding. In all your ways acknowledge him, and he will make straight your paths. ~ Proverbs 3:5-6

Faith is the courage to treat everything that happens as exactly what you need for your HIGHEST good and learning.

Now faith is the assurance of things hoped for, the conviction of things not seen.
~ Hebrews 11:1

Emotional swells are a normal part of daily life. Ride the waves of your emotions. As waves change, so your emotions will change. Stay steady and centered through it all. Place your attention on peaceful thoughts and hold love constantly in your heart. Love in your mind and love in your heart overcomes negativity in the world.

I have said these things to you, that in me you may have peace. In the world you will have tribulation. But take heart; I have overcome the world. ~ John 16:33

Don't sit around today asking, "What is the meaning of life?" The meaning of life can be found only in LIVING life to its FULLEST!

Delight yourself in the Lord, and he will give you the desires of your heart. ~ Psalm 37:4

A woman knows that her power comes from the balance and flexibility of being in tune with her emotions as well as her intelligence. She is graceful yet fierce, strong yet supple in her ways.

Strength and dignity are her clothing, and she laughs at the time to come.
~ Proverbs 31:25

Nothing in our experience goes away until it has taught us what we need to know and embody.

Let the wise hear and increase in learning, and the one who understands obtain guidance. ~ Proverbs 1:5

Even when our culture teaches us to be afraid, reach out in love. Even when everyone else is ready to judge and throw stones (harm), make a way for understanding, peace and safety for all beings. As a child of God (Love), be like the living God, the God who IS Love. Love others without fear or judgment.

There is no fear in love, but perfect love casts out fear. For fear has to do with punishment, and whoever fears has not been perfected in love. ~ 1 John 4:18

I am in COMPLETE and total LOVE with today, with LIFE and with all that is. Beauty is everywhere and in everything. I can feel love LIFTING my HEART!

So we have come to know and to believe the love that God has for us. God is love, and whoever abides in love abides in God, and God abides in him. ~ 1 John 4:16

Make the most of what happens in your life (both good and bad) and grab that pearl of wisdom from your experience. There is no better teacher than life itself. It is the nature of life that we face our darkest hour before we are able to see the light of our brightest truth.

Even the darkness is not dark to you; the night is bright as the day, for darkness is as light with you. ~ Psalm 139:12

Perfection is our natural state. It's not through performance, it's about "being" who we already are!

You therefore must be perfect, as your heavenly Father is perfect. ~ Matthew 5:48

It is essential to love and give all beings your gift of love, time and attention. Money and material goods don't last forever, but the memories of love, friendship and connection are eternal.

Set your minds on things that are above, not on things that are on earth. ~ Colossians 3:2

Your kindness will inspire kindness in others.

Think kindly!

Speak kindly!

Act kindly!

She opens her mouth with wisdom, and the teaching of kindness is on her tongue.
~ Proverbs 31:26

When we believe in our goals and feel them from our soul, we create unlimited possibilities to be realized. We shed our fear of the impossible and open our heart, mind and spirit to the possible!

For nothing will be impossible with God.
~ Luke 1:37

Your life experiences are the result of all your daily thoughts and choices. You can choose to look for LOVE (God Opportunities) in the face of adversity or you can let negative influences bring you down. The way you choose to perceive the world creates the world that you experience.

Now is the time to release any negative or limiting beliefs that no longer support your passage. Focus on developing empowering thoughts that are aligned with the spirit of love. Focus on values that instill love, beliefs that support love, goal's that inspire love and choices that foster love.

In all your ways acknowledge him, and he will make straight your paths.
~ Proverbs 3:6

When we commit from our heart, we commit to something we believe in by aligning our will with the power of love. We commit to an ideal, a standard and a way of life that supports a higher calling to love, joy, peace and compassion for all beings.

See what kind of love the Father has given to us, that we should be called children of God; and so we are. ~ 1 John 3:1

Being a generous giver and a gracious receiver is the highest call to Love. Blessings and offerings help restore our sense of belonging to the Whole.

Let the moon and the tides remind us, in the wisdom of their rising and falling, pushing and pulling, that we are advised to do the same.

Give and receive with love, give and receive with joy, give and receive without attachment, without expectation and you will receive fulfillment, happiness and the highest call to love in the light of well-being.

Give, and it will be given to you. Good measure, pressed down, shaken together, running over, will be put into your lap. For with the measure you use it will be measured back to you. ~ Luke 6:38

When we see each other eye to eye, we are really seeing each other soul to soul.

No one has ever seen God; if we love one another, God abides in us and his love is perfected in us. ~ 1 John 4:12

All it takes to be lovely is to wear a lovely smile. Share your smile with the world and the world smiles and shines upon you with love, beauty and grace.

The Lord make his face to shine upon you and be gracious to you. ~ Numbers 6:25

Everything is an "idea" in the mind of God (Love). Let your every idea be a benevolent blessing of love, joy, peace, compassion and well-being!

By faith we understand that the universe was created by the word of God, so that what is seen was not made out of things that are visible. ~ Hebrews 11:3

God (The Infinite Intelligence) is not the creator of negativity, judgment or fearful thinking but we are when we allow our thoughts to be anything but loving, encouraging and kind towards each other and ourselves! When we believe in anything but Love and well-being we conform to a world thought system based in fear, negativity and judgment.

Love resurrects our heart and restores the integrity of our mind!

When we no longer allow negativity or fearful thinking to permeate our mind we return to our heavenly home where everything is good, acceptable, perfect and purified in Love.

Welcome to the new world (the new life, the new heaven, the new mind)!

Do not be conformed to this world, but be transformed by the renewal of your mind, that by testing you may discern what is the will of God, what is good and acceptable and perfect. ~ Romans 12:2

No one can depress you.
No one can make you anxious.
No one can hurt your feelings.
No one can make you anything other than what you "allow" inside.

If you feel that someone is hurting you emotionally, take a deep breath, feel the feeling, and then remind yourself that you won't "allow" his or her words to affect your well being. When you feed into negativity, you teach others that they can depend on you for a reaction.

This is what is meant by turn the other cheek. When you can remain peaceful by not giving others the power to affect you, you place your attention on a higher power (Love) instead of negativity, hate and blame.

You have heard that it was said, 'Eye for eye, and tooth for tooth.' But I tell you, do not resist an evil person. If anyone slaps you on the right cheek, turn to them the other cheek also. ~ Matthew 5:38-39

Life doesn't always move in a straight or perfect line but usually zigzags. There are going to be peaks, valleys, twists, turns, trials and tribulations in our human experience – there is no getting around it. No matter how great everything appears to be on the outside, we all experience the ups and downs of daily life. The most important thing is to create contentment in your heart and peace of mind in your daily thought process to establish well-being as a way of life.

Enjoy prosperity while you can, but when hard times strike, realize that both come from God. Remember that nothing is certain in this life. ~ Ecclesiastes 7:14

God is our heavenly creator and is Pure Love in Spirit.

Christ the Son is Pure Love in Spirit.

Christ was given to us as a physical example of what Pure Love "is" and shows us exactly what Pure Love looks like.

Christ is Pure Love, walking.

His love lesson to humanity was to show us how to walk in Love.

The only way to our father (our heavenly creator) is "through" Love.

We must follow Christ's example and walk in Love daily.

Humanity can only come to know our Creator (our heavenly father) through the Spirit of Love.

I believe in Love!

For God so loved the world, that he gave his only Son, that whoever believes in him should not perish but have eternal life.

~ John 3:16

Don't allow material attire to dictate your worth. Clothe yourself in Love and you will be well dressed for life!

And above all these put on love, which binds everything together in perfect harmony.
~ Colossians 3:14

Our lives are so full of things that rob our soul of peace and inner-reflection. We don't take enough time out each day to think about personal growth and well-being. The noise and distractions of everyday life are constant; TV, work, computers, cell phones, etc . . . all crowd our thoughts and leave us no time for self-reflection. Don't allow the "junk" in life to control you.

Take some time out to ponder your life, think about the person you are and the person you want to become. The investment of quiet reflection will pay off down the road in great dividends. Prayer and daily meditation are effective ways to refresh your spirit and rejuvenate your mind.

Listen to me in silence, O coastlands; let the peoples renew their strength. ~ Isaiah 41

It is not our painful experiences that hurt us most; it is our resistance to them that wears us out. It takes a lot more energy to store our pain than it does to confront it head on.

The night racks my bones, and the pain that gnaws me takes no rest. ~ Job 30:17

Some people come into our lives to make a lasting impression and then quietly fade away.

Some people come into our lives to penetrate our souls, wake us up and move our heart towards love.

Some people come into our lives in order to broaden our understanding, impart wisdom and provide guidance.

Some people come into our lives in order to wound us so that we can learn the importance of trust and forgiveness while also being cautious to whom we open our hearts to.

Some people come into our lives in order to make the days more beautiful, to enrich our spirits and to leave a footprint on our hearts.

We don't know what we have in these people until we lose them and we don't know what we have been missing until they arrive.

So be grateful for each person that comes

into your life as they bestow a blessing and a purpose.

I will instruct you and teach you in the way you should go; I will counsel you with my eye upon you. ~ Psalm 32:8

Always know that great good can come from great bad. Exquisitely beautiful things can come from the plain ugly things in life. Never discount or devalue the flower that emerges from the soil. In fact, this makes the flower all the more healthy, precious and beautiful. Always focus on the flower (your blessings) and be grateful for the soil (your adversities) that facilitates the expansion towards your greatest good (Glory)!

Be strong and courageous. Do not be frightened, and do not be dismayed, for the LORD your God is with you wherever you go. ~ Joshua 1:9

Our words have power. Power to hurt and power to heal. Angry words spill from an angry heart. A loving person speaks gracious words of love, compassion and goodness. May your words build others up, not tear them down, bless rather than curse, encourage not discourage.

Let no corrupting talk come out of your mouths, but only such as is good for building up, as fits the occasion, that it may give grace to those who hear. ~ Ephesians 4:29

Right now is all about living like there is no tomorrow. Beauty is everywhere, in every moment, in your every activity. You have been blessed with this instant, and this one, and this one, and this one…. These precious moments will only happen once so be fully present for them. Catch them, savor them, relish them. Live each "God Loving Moment" with joy in your soul and gratitude in your heart!

You make known to me the path of life; in your presence there is fullness of joy; at your right hand are pleasures forevermore.
~ Psalm 16:11

Revenge is a sure-fire way to let someone know that they got the best of you. Don't give your power away! Instead re-channel your energy into moving forward and the rest will take care of itself.

See that no one repays anyone evil for evil, but always seek to do good to one another and to everyone. ~ 1 Thessalonians 5:15

Temptation is when something makes us want to do something that we feel is wrong. The good news is that temptation is not a bad thing!

Temptation is a signal, a red flag, a feeling from "within" that forewarns us what we are contemplating is not right, so that we can choose differently.

Everyone is tempted from time to time but we all have free choice to choose a more productive path. Temptation is a gift of the spirit. It brings us the gift of "awareness" so that we don't have to suffer through a negative or painful experience.

No temptation has overtaken you that is not common to man. God is faithful, and he will not let you be tempted beyond your ability, but with the temptation he will also provide the way of escape, that you may be able to endure it. ~ 1 Corinthians 10:13

Do something that you love, create something that you believe in and live your life with purpose and passion. Do that, and it won't matter how much money you make!

Whatever you do, work heartily, as for the Lord and not for men. ~ Colossians 3:23

When other people act in ways that you want them to act you feel happy, pleased, joyful and satisfied but when they don't act in ways that you want them to act you feel, disappointed, resentful, agitated, betrayed and maybe even devalued in some way.

This is because relationship (of any kind) is a place where we each encounter unhealed emotions in ourselves that need to be healed. Relationships are an opportunity for self-growth and they offer a domain to explore all of our unhealed emotions along with the ability to observe our reactions to our emotions.

Relationship to one another gives us the opportunity to address and change any unhealed emotions that are keeping us from realizing our highest and most loving selves. Every person in our life is here to help us grow closer to Love (God) if we allow ourselves to change and heal for the better.

Complete my joy by being of the same mind, having the same love, being in full accord and of one mind. ~ Philippians 2:2

When attracting friends and loved ones into your life pay less attention to what they say than to what they do. Take note of things like: Do they live a lifestyle that you respect? Are they kind, compassionate, balanced, healthy, honest, open, respectful? Do they have a good sense of humor? If not, move on to someone more inspiring. It's always best to attract people who display a positive influence in their thoughts, words, actions and deeds.

Whoever walks with the wise becomes wise, but the companion of fools will suffer harm.
~ Proverbs 13:20

You are a mirror of Love, in which God (Love) shines forth perfect light into the world. The sun is not afraid to shine its light - nor should you be afraid to shine your light! In Truth, it's all God's Light anyway so believe in the Light and shine in the Love!

While you have the light, believe in the light, that you may become sons of light.
~ John 12:36

Your job is not to find your purpose – your job is to "serve" a purpose, and then your purpose will serve you.

And we know that for those who love God all things work together for good, for those who are called according to his purpose.
~ Romans 8:28

One of the most loving acts of kindness any of us can do in life is to reach out and do a good deed for another human being.

In all things I have shown you that by working hard in this way we must help the weak and remember the words of the Lord Jesus, how he himself said, "It is more blessed to give than to receive." ~ Acts 20:35

Our goals are like precious pearls of creation. They are rare, valuable and prized. Our goals should be cultivated, nurtured and tended until they come to full fruition for our highest calling.

Prepare your work outside; get everything ready for yourself in the field, and after that build your house. ~ Proverbs 24:27

When we are living from a state of JOY - joy becomes the living evidence of the spirit within us. Joy is the active quality of our awareness and our whole being is therefore secure.

Therefore my heart is glad, and my whole being rejoices; my flesh also dwells secure.
~ Psalm 16:9

By lifting or opening your heart to God (Love) you are connecting to the higher wisdom of the Holy Spirit (which is your intuition, internal guidance system and direct communication link to God).

When you connect to your higher wisdom, you will never go wrong. The Holy Spirit gives us the "gift" of knowledge to solve our problems and the problems that weigh heavily upon family and friends. Listening, acting and speaking from this Loving Guidance will always bring you peace of mind, sound direction and contentment of heart.

And the Spirit of the LORD shall rest upon him, the Spirit of wisdom and understanding, the Spirit of counsel and might, the Spirit of knowledge and the fear of the LORD. ~ Isaiah 11:2

To see abundance with your eyesight – you first have to "feel" it with your insight.

But the meek shall inherit the land and delight themselves in abundant peace.
~ Psalm 37:11

Looking at our past experiences gives us the opportunity to create a better life for ourselves. We have the power to let go of our old story in favor of creating and living a better one!

By accepting our past and learning from it, we can move forward in a positive light by rewriting the script that no longer defines us.

Let your eyes look directly forward, and your gaze be straight before you. Ponder the path of your feet; then all your ways will be sure.
~ Proverbs 4:25-27

Cultivating a "healthy" relationship is one of the most honorable things you can do for yourself and your beloved.

Trust, intimacy, respect, honesty, faith and open communication are the bricks that offer a sound structure and allow it to flourish into a glorious and loving merger.

All that is required is that our love be pure.

Let love be genuine. ~ Romans 12:9

In this journey called life, storms will arise even if we can't see them on the horizon.

So, it's always best to take charge and prepare for the storms (challenges in life), instead of being overwhelmed (flooded) by them when they arrive.

If we are going to live with significance in this world, we are going to have to accept and embrace all adversity as an opportunity to grow spiritually stronger rather than something to be overwhelmed (flooded) by.

By faith Noah, being warned by God concerning events as yet unseen, in reverent fear constructed an ark for the saving of his household. ~ Hebrews 11:7

Victorious people change their world from within instead of expecting the world to change around them to meet their expectations.

Behold! I tell you a mystery. We shall not all sleep, but we shall all be changed.
~ 1 Corinthians 15:51

Our expansion does not come from a mind that is thinking and analyzing about what to do or say but rather from a mind that empties itself into the heart of God. In this way, the consciousness of God (Love) can shine through our human form unencumbered.

And I will give them one heart, and a new spirit I will put within them. ~ Ezekiel 11:19

We will know the instant that we have embraced the lessons from all of our painful experiences here on earth the moment we decide to change our thoughts.

We choose to change our thoughts because we do not want to relive those painful experiences over and over and over again!

When we decide to change our thoughts for the better, our painful experiences will change for the better.

This will not happen until we make the connection between our thoughts, our actions and our life experiences (our self-created outcomes).

Create in me a clean heart, O God, and renew a right spirit within me.
~ Psalm 51:10-12

So many people were never properly taught how to receive because it has been conditioned out of them.

Because of this, receiving is a skill that needs to be relearned in order to give back freely.

Let your heart know that it is OK to receive without guilt.

When you become a gracious receiver, you are opening up to the flow of joy that is always flowing to us from the Source of Love.

When you receive a blessing, you are also giving the flow of joy back to the giver through your willingness to accept Love's gift.

The flow of giving AND receiving is a complete circle of joy TO You FROM Love and FROM You TO Love.

And we are writing these things so that our joy may be complete. ~ 1 John 1:4

In the context of relationship, it is no one's job to bring love "to" us.

True relationship is the way we equally participate in the field of love.

We are not called forth to complete each other, we are called forth to reveal our completeness and wholeness as one body and one spirit.

There is one body and one Spirit—just as you were called to the one hope that belongs to your call. ~ Ephesians 4:4

The less you magnify and take on what others say about you personally, the happier you will be.

You will know when you have succeeded in not taking what others say about you personally when you no longer feel the need to defend yourself.

When you begin to realize that others are conveying something about themselves, even though they're directing their comments towards you. This is when you will know that you are getting the hang of not letting their negative comments affect you.

Be sober-minded. Be watchful. ~ 1 Peter 5:8

Choose to become conscious of not allowing negative emotions and feelings to build up inside of you when you are angry or disappointed with someone.

Be sure to always express your feelings openly and honestly so that you will free yourself from emotional pain, struggle and inner turmoil.

If you are resisting interaction from others through the act of withdrawal, avoidance and/or silence, understand that you are repeating old patterns stemming from early experiences of rejection, fear, mistrust and insecurity that need to be healed.

When you shut down emotionally, you are choosing to shut out the higher vibrations of love, unity, joy. Don't shut out the light from entering!

If a kingdom is divided against itself, that kingdom cannot stand. ~ Mark 3:24

Living life in the Spirit of Love is the Way to our Heavenly Father. Love by its very nature cannot divide nor discriminate. Love doesn't see the color of our skin, our gender or even our religious affiliation. Love is for every one of us without exception. The Spirit of Love is universal by design. Living life in the Spirit of Love (Christ) is the way to peace, truth and light.

I and the Father are one. ~ John 10:30

When we allow "abundant consciousness" to be fully present in our thoughts, our hearts overflow with richness.

We realize that we have everything we need from within our being so we no longer attach ourselves to consumerism or lend debt to the world of materialism.

Instead, we give our coin (belief) to God (the Higher Intelligence) knowing that there is no lack of anything within a Universe that is living, eternal, abundant and fully prosperous!

The rich rules over the poor, and the borrower is servant to the lender.
~ Proverbs 22:7

Focus on the things, people and events that are critical to your joy and well-being. Set your attention and priorities on the things that really matter!

When you determine your priorities, you will discover that deep down, they are the measures you use to determine if your life is turning out the way you want it to.

But test everything; hold fast what is good.
~ 1 Thessalonians 5:21

Don't worry about being a successful person, instead, be a good person and do good work and success will follow you in good measure!

Humble yourselves before the Lord, and he will exalt you. ~ James 4:10

Positive people are beautiful beams of light and they make a cheerful impression wherever they go!

To be a positive person you act in positive ways, even if it's not always how you feel.

Think and speak positively to yourself and others, act happy, act confident, act joyful and believe in yourself because acting out an emotion is what "awakens" the emotion from "within."

May the God of hope fill you with all joy and peace in believing, so that by the power of the Holy Spirit you may abound in hope.
~ Romans 15:13

Fear is not all of who you are, rather it is an emotion that you are experiencing.

Daily living is not about how to avoid fear, but how to make positive decisions that strengthen your faith while fear is present.

*He is not afraid of bad news; his heart is firm, trusting in the L*ORD*. His heart is steady; he will not be afraid, until he looks in triumph on his adversaries. ~ Psalm 112:7-8*

When you surround yourself with people who treat you with respect, you will find that the basis for their respect is the respect that you have towards yourself and so towards others.

This is because when you respect yourself, you believe that you are a worthy individual and deserving of respect, not just from yourself but from everyone else.

Show yourself in all respects to be a model of good works, and in your teaching show integrity, dignity, respect. ~ Titus 2:7

By eating healthy foods and aligning your heart with the "Higher Intelligence" you can enjoy knowing that you are giving your body, mind and spirit all the nutrients it needs to protect and enhance its healing ability.

You shall serve the Lord your God, and he will bless your bread and your water, and I will take sickness away from among you.
~ Exodus 23:25

Your personality and character are perfectly suited for the needs of your soul. Be at peace with who you already ARE. Everything is working for your highest good.

Do you not know that you are God's temple and that God's Spirit dwells in you?
~ 1 Corinthians 3:16

Spirit is pure, and all our life experiences are helping us to grow and merge into that same Love.

Blessed are the pure in heart, for they shall see God. ~ Matthew 5:8

There is a great joy in becoming free and letting go of a situation, person or thing that no longer supports us in a positive way.

Instead of focusing on what you are losing by letting go, realize that you are gaining something more wonderful that will lead you into a better life.

Just as a caterpillar must struggle before it becomes a butterfly, we often are faced with a similar process in our own transformation.

When we give way to freedom - we understand how wonderful it is to take flight.

Remember not the former things, nor consider the things of old. Behold, I am doing a new thing; now it springs forth, do you not perceive it? I will make a way in the wilderness and rivers in the desert.
~ Isaiah 43:18-19

Forgiveness centers us in the present moment. Forgiveness doesn't change what happened, it changes our view of what happened.

As we release our need to hold onto past wounds, we feel a surge of peace within our being and in relationship to the world around us.

We give flight to freedom when we choose forgiveness because we focus our attention on the present, and let go of the past.

For I will forgive their iniquity, and I will remember their sin no more.
~ Jeremiah 31:34

Happiness is something that you are and it comes from the way you think.

You are being renewed in the spirit of your minds. ~ Ephesians 4:23

Find a quiet moment of peace in your day and you will create a sense of well-being in your heart.

Now may the Lord of peace himself give you peace at all times in every way.
~ 2 Thessalonians 3:16

Practicing Gratitude daily is nothing more than practicing Love daily.

For where your treasure is, there your heart will be also. ~ Matthew 6:21

People can rationalize doing almost anything they set their mind to, but God (Love) looks beyond rationalization to the motives of the heart.

People may be right in their own eyes, but the Lord examines the heart. ~ Proverbs 21:2

We are all born to co-create with God (Love) by extending the energy of love, creativity, joy, well-being, kindness and compassion to one another. These are the commandments of God's Love.

If you love me, you will keep my commandments. ~ John 14:15

The Spirit of Love teaches us how to communicate from a state of compassion, not a place of judgment.

Do not speak evil against one another, brothers. The one who speaks against a brother or judges his brother, speaks evil against the law and judges the law. But if you judge the law, you are not a doer of the law but a judge. There is only one lawgiver and judge, he who is able to save and to destroy. But who are you to judge your neighbor? ~ James 4:11-12

Healing can only occur when our deep emotional wounds are revealed and then purified in the Light of Pure Love (God).

Behold, I will bring to it health and healing, and I will heal them and reveal to them abundance of prosperity and security.
~ Jeremiah 33:6

Don't allow the negative people in your life to steal your joy or make you miserable.

The thief comes only to steal and kill and destroy; I have come that they may have life, and have it to the full. ~ John 10:10

Stand strong in your joy, hold true to your faith and the blessings of happiness and peace will be yours forever.

Finally, my brethren, be strong in the Lord, and in the power of his might.
~ Ephesians 6:10-17

Stop worrying about what others think of you because in truth, others rarely do.

It is dangerous to be concerned with what others think of you. ~ Proverbs 29:25

When you see beauty in another soul, you are seeing your own soul's beauty. When you are helping another, you are seeing them as yourself, as part of the whole.

So then, as we have opportunity, let us do good to everyone, and especially to those who are of the household of faith.
~ Galatians 6:10

When you assume responsibility for your experiences, through your conscious choices, your life becomes meaningful.

Responsible choice is the healing dynamic that removes your fears from having power over you.

Responsibility is not a burden you must carry, but a doorway to your freedom.

For each will have to bear his own load.
~ Galatians 6:5

Your only task is to stay centered in God (Love).

Let all that you do be done in love.
~ 1 Corinthians 16:14

When you feel unconditional love emanating from someone, it mirrors the unconditional love within yourself, otherwise you would not be aware of this love energy.

Anyone who does not love does not know God, because God is love. ~ 1 John 4:8

Be READY, God (Love) is preparing you for Higher Ground!

Therefore you also must be ready, for the Son of Man is coming at an hour you do not expect. ~ Matthew 24:44

Be a warrior of FAITH, not a worrier of FEAR!

You will be secure, because there is hope; you will look about you and take your rest in safety. ~ Job 11:18

God (Love) is like the wind. You can't see Him but you can definitely feel Her power blowing through you!

By this we know that we abide in him and he in us, because he has given us of his Spirit. ~ 1 John 4:13

LOVE is the greatest of all human qualities, and it is an attribute of God. Love involves service to others; to show it gives evidence that you care.

FAITH is trusting that the Divine Intelligence dwells within us.

HOPE is the ability to keep focusing on the good.

LOVE is taking right action.

Three things will last forever—faith, hope, and love—and the greatest of these is love.
~ Corinthians 13:13

NEVER be afraid to LOVE - be afraid NOT to!

Hatred stirs up strife, but love covers all offenses. ~ Proverbs 10:12

Nurture your friendships. They are angels supporting your flight!

Oil and perfume make the heart glad, and the sweetness of a friend comes from his earnest counsel. ~ Proverbs 27:9

We are all extensions of God's (Love), just as rays of light are the extensions of the sun that originate from the same Source. We are here to shine our light into the world!

No one lights a lamp and then puts it under a basket. Instead, a lamp is placed on a stand, where it gives light to everyone in the house. ~ Matthew 5:15

At some point each evening, take a moment to reflect on all the blessings you have received for the day. Consider how you can take those blessings into your HEART and radiate them out towards others.

And from his fullness we have all received, grace upon grace. ~ John 1:16

You are never done until you quit trying.

Don't ever give up, instead, GET UP and press into the new magnificent beginning that God (Love) has in store for you!

And let us not grow weary of doing good, for in due season we will reap, if we do not give up. ~ Galatians 6:9

You can overcome any obstacle and any challenge that faces you. So never give up! You have the Spirit of God (Love) inside of you!

I have fought the good fight, I have finished the race, I have kept the faith.
~ 2 Timothy 4:7

Don't waste the rest of your life energy feeling bad about something you wish you could change or do over. It's NEVER too late to begin again!

And though your beginning was small, your latter days will be very great. ~ Job 8:7

Meditate on the things that God (Love), wants you to hear and NOT on the negative things that trivial people want you to hear.

I will meditate on your precepts and fix my eyes on your ways. ~ Psalm 119:15

God (Love) The Infinite Intelligence is on your side! Always has been and always will be!

For I know the plans I have for you, declares the Lord, plans for welfare and not for evil, to give you a future and a hope.
~ Jeremiah 29:11

It's not always easy to forgive people who have hurt you but it's so much easier than staying bitter in your heart and allowing them to affect your entire life in an unhealthy way.

Hatred stirs up strife, but love covers all offenses. ~ Proverbs 10:12

Don't settle for anything LESS than the VERY BEST LIFE that God (Love) The Infinite Intelligence has for you!

Blessed is the man who remains steadfast under trial, for when he has stood the test he will receive the crown of life, which God has promised to those who love him.
~ James 1:12

Even the most hurtful things you have experienced have made you a stronger, more resilient person. It may help to remember that you are who you are because of EVERYTHING that has happened to you... good and bad alike.

More than that, we rejoice in our sufferings, knowing that suffering produces endurance.
~ Romans 5:3

God (The Infinite Intelligence) is "always" working for your greater good!

Foster a perspective where you see the potential in everyone and in everything. A brighter perspective where you believe in the "BEST" more than you do the worst.

A perspective where you realize Abundance is everywhere and in every thing and is well within your reach!

Bless our God, O peoples; let the sound of his praise be heard, who has kept our soul among the living and has not let our feet slip. For you, O God, have tested us; you have tried us as silver is tried. You brought us into the net; you laid a crushing burden on our backs; you let men ride over our heads; we went through fire and through water; yet you have brought us out to a place of abundance.
~ Psalm 66:8

As unique individuals, our differences aren't any better or any worse, they're just beautifully different and equally beautiful.

There is neither Jew nor Greek, there is neither slave nor free, there is no male and female, for you are all one in Christ Jesus.
~ Galatians 3:28

The word "Yes" in any language is one of the most powerful words you can use. It will instantaneously and naturally expand your energy field, and make you more receptive to what God (The Infinite Intelligence) is offering you.

When you say "Yes" it creates a powerful resonance in your HEART sending out love and positive vibrations into the world.

After this I heard what seemed to be the loud voice of a great multitude in heaven, crying out, "Hallelujah! Salvation and glory and power belong to our God." ~ Revelation 19:1

Making mistakes is a part of life. You can't be afraid of making mistakes or you'll never learn to play a bigger game!

Fear not, for I am with you; be not dismayed, for I am your God; I will strengthen you, I will help you, I will uphold you with my righteous right hand. ~ Isaiah 41:10

Keep moving courageously forward in your faith!

Focus all your attention on how God (The Infinite Intelligence) has already blessed your life, and you will find courage and strength filling your heart.

For God gave us a spirit not of fear but of power and love and self-control.
~ 2 Timothy 1:7

We will never stop wanting more until we allow ourselves to be at peace with what we already have.

Whoever loves money never has enough; whoever loves wealth is never satisfied with their income. This too is meaningless.
~ Ecclesiastes 5:10

Failure is not bad, it is just "feedback" for positive change.

My flesh and my heart may fail, but God is the strength of my heart and my portion forever. ~ Psalm 73:26

Love is the greatest of all human qualities, and it is an attribute of God. Love involves service to others; to show it gives evidence that you care.

The Spirit of Love teaches us how to communicate from a state of compassion, not a place of judgment. In this place, we are healed.

When he went ashore he saw a great crowd, and he had compassion on them and healed their sick. ~ Matthew 14:14

You don't always need a precise plan. Sometimes you just need to take a deep breath, trust in God (The Infinite Intelligence), let go and be grateful for all the blessings that are coming your way!

When I am afraid, I put my trust in you. In God, whose word I praise, in God I trust; I shall not be afraid. What can flesh do to me?
~ Psalm 56:3-4

It's not about fixing something in your life that's broken, its' about acquiring a new perspective and creating something in your life that's even MORE BEAUTIFUL!

Out of Zion, the perfection of beauty, God shines forth. ~ Psalm 50:2

As we LOVE and communicate with the BEST in people - they reflect our love, and the whole world changes one SMILE at a time!

Beloved, let us love one another, for love is from God, and whoever loves has been born of God and knows God. ~ 1 John 4:7

If you want to make a real and lasting CHANGE in how you FEEL from within, you've got to turn off the self-criticism and choose to be GENTLE with yourself. And every time you do, it will be one step closer to matching the ENERGY of your desires and ATTRACTING what you want out of life. This will be in direct alignment with Gods perfect will for you.

But seek first the kingdom of God and his righteousness, and all these things will be added to you. ~ Matthew 6:33

We all have talents and attributes that make us wonderful and gifted human beings and we ALL can demonstrate this in any body size, shape, color and ethnicity!

But the fruit of the Spirit is love, joy, peace, patience, kindness, goodness, faithfulness, gentleness, self-control; against such things there is no law. ~ Galatians 5:22-23

When we make a loving difference in the world - that's what counts the most!

Therefore be imitators of God, as beloved children. And walk in love, as Christ loved us and gave himself up for us, a fragrant offering and sacrifice to God.
~ Ephesians 5:1-2

Our relationships are our greatest blessings. Treasure the ones you love as being your greatest asset because they are.

Above all, keep loving one another earnestly, since love covers a multitude of sins.
~ 1 Peter 4:8

The essence of God (Love) lives within each one of us and our love, commitment and kindness to one another is our living testament.

A new commandment I give to you, that you love one another: just as I have loved you, you also are to love one another.
~ John 13:34

When you are doing what you love, you listen to your intuition, you take actions driven by what you love, you follow your heart, passions and you express your unique gifts and talents to the world without fear.

But the Helper, the Holy Spirit, whom the Father will send in my name, he will teach you all things and bring to your remembrance all that I have said to you.
~ John 14:26

Being love is about seeing the world, others and everything in your life through the eyes of love – no judgement or criticism.

Jesus said to him, "I am the way, and the truth, and the life." ~ John 14:6

Nothing is too good to be true and nothing is too good to last when you look to God (Love) for your good.

*The L*ORD *is good to those who wait for him,
to the soul who seeks him.
~ Lamentations 3:25*

Seeking advice from people you trust that have your best interest at heart is wise council in times of confusion, stress or uncertainty. God (Love) communicates to us with the help, aid and support of others who maintain a positive and loving influence in our life.

Without counsel plans fail, but with many advisers they succeed. ~ Proverbs 15:22

When we allow ourselves to think negatively, we damage our potential in so many ways. The worst thing is that we may be so wrapped up in our own negativity that we cannot even see that there are ways out of this darkness.

However, there is always a choice. Once you become aware of your negative thoughts - then you can decide which type of thoughts you want to focus on to see the positive light.

To give light to those who sit in darkness and in the shadow of death, to guide our feet into the way of peace. ~ Luke 1:79

I will watch my thoughts - as my thoughts become my feelings.

I will watch my feelings - as my feelings become my actions.

I will watch my actions - as my actions become my outcomes.

I will watch my outcomes - as my outcomes determine my destiny.

Commit your work to the LORD, and your plans will be established. ~ Proverbs 16:3

Give and receive with love.

Give and receive with joy.

Give and receive without attachment.

Give and receive without expectation.

You shall give to him freely, and your heart shall not be grudging when you give to him, because for this the LORD your God will bless you in all your work and in all that you undertake. ~ Deuteronomy 15:10

Doing good and displaying acts of kindness is essential to our well-being. Giving without expectation with no need to be repaid is the most powerful act of generosity we can offer.

Good heartedness can lead us wherever we want to go - to a happier life and making a positive difference in the world.

And let us consider how to stir up one another to love and good works.
~ Hebrews 10:24

When you are living your authentic truth, you are growing, you are empowered and you are a light to others. You are joyful, because you are being genuine and taking responsibility for your life and being in service to something greater than yourself.

The greatest work that each of us can undertake each day is our own inner work and self-development. We need to begin the process of truly knowing ourselves deeply. We need to pay attention to our thoughts, detect our largest values and define how we wish to conduct our life. Inner discovery is a lifelong journey and our work here on earth is never done until our last breath. By being true to yourself, you will be free to experience the Divinity within you.

And you will know the truth, and the truth will set you free. ~ John 8:32

About the Author

Gena Livings is a spiritual practitioner of peaceful living and the founder of GenaLivings.com.

Gena radically redesigned her life after spending eighteen years in a high-stress corporate environment that left her body and spirit utterly depleted. She studied anatomy, physiology, pathology, sports medicine, nutrition, lifestyle modification coaching, and fitness training before obtaining her certification as a personal trainer and health and wellness professional.

Today Gena does what she loves by expressing herself through writing and inspiring others to achieve a lifestyle that promotes health and well-being as a better way of life. As a wellness writer and a spiritual practitioner of peaceful living, she helps people cultivate their awareness so that they can make conscious lifestyle choices based on healthy lifestyle practices and a healthy mind-set.

Other Books Written by Gena:

- *Saturdays With Bob: Life Changing Golf Lessons for Mind, Body and Spirit*

- *Eat Healthy for Balance and Wholeness – A Conscious Food Guide for Building Awareness and Honoring Your Body Temple*

- A FREE online hand-guide entitled "Inspired Wellness – The Livings Key Principles for Creating Wholeness, Peace and Health From the Inside Out"

Be sure to connect with Gena at: GenaLivings.com

www.ingramcontent.com/pod-product-compliance
Lightning Source LLC
Chambersburg PA
CBHW051759040426
42446CB00007B/441